THE MONEY CONNECTOR™

HOW TO MAKE AN INCOME LENDING OTHER PEOPLE'S MONEY

LEE ARNOLD

Earnings Disclaimer: We make every effort to ensure that we accurately represent our products and services and their potential for income. . Our programs are not designed or intended to qualify individuals for employment. Our programs are avocational in nature and are intended for the purpose of the personal enrichment, development, and enjoyment of individuals. Earning and Income statements made by our company and its customers are supplied directly from the customer. There is no guarantee that you will make these levels of income — in fact, most people do not — and you accept the risk that the earnings and income statements differ by individual.

As with any business, your results may vary, and will be based on your individual capacity, business experience, expertise, and level of desire. There are no guarantees concerning the level of success you may experience. The testimonials and examples used are not intended to represent or guarantee that anyone will achieve the same or similar results. Each individual's success depends on his or her background, dedication, desire and motivation.

There is no assurance that examples of past earnings can be duplicated in the future. We cannot guarantee your future results and/or success. There are some unknown risks in business and on the internet that we cannot foresee which can reduce results. We are not responsible for your actions.

The use of our information, products and services should be based on your own due diligence and you agree that our company is not liable for any success or failure of your business that is directly or indirectly related to the purchase and use of our information, products and services.

Lending is not available where prohibited by law, or in states where Cogo Capital does not trade. Loans are available only on non-owner occupied real property. NMLS #1760709; Arizona Mortgage Broker License #0950084; California Finance Lenders License 60DBO-101344. Loans are also available in California through Cogo Capital Orange County, Inc. – California DRE License #01928542; NMLS #1051036. You may access more information about Cogo Capital at the NMLS Consumer Access Page. Cogo Capital Underwriting Guidelines are subject to change without notice. COGO CAPITAL SHALL BE UNDER NO OBLIGATION TO FUND ANY LOAN TO ANY BORROWER UNLESS AND UNTIL IT IS SATISFIED, IN ITS SOLE AND ABSOLUTE DISCRETION, WITH ITS DUE DILIGENCE REVIEW AND FORMAL LOAN DOCUMENTS PREPARED BY ITS COUNSEL.

TABLE OF CONTENTS

INTRODUCTION

Volatile financial markets have had a hectic effect on nearly every aspect of our daily lives, but one of the most surprising developments involves the investing world. People have recently been hit with nonstop news reports about novice investors flooding the stock market. This has led to some crazy action in the markets, sometimes sending worthless stocks "to the moon" before they bottomed out and took countless investors' savings with them. It was a little disheartening seeing so many people lose money on these investments when I knew there was a better way.

Around the same time people were souring on "meme stocks" – or maybe partially because of that disenchantment – Americans seemed to discover that it was better to invest in real estate than in the stock market. Of course, this wasn't necessarily new. A recent CNBC headline declared, *"Americans down on stocks, say real estate is best investment."* A year after that article came out, MarketWatch released a report saying, *"Americans think it's better to invest in housing than the stock market."*

The fact is Americans know that real estate is a prime investment. Unfortunately, it's not always easy to break into this world. Or, at least, it seems that way. Most people view the prospect of buying their own home as so complex that they need a real estate agent. If people think that's difficult, imagine what they think about investing in real estate. It's no wonder so many people shy away from the market. But what if I told you that getting into this industry doesn't have to involve complex processes or even purchasing property?

If I've already snagged you on the idea that complexity isn't an issue, maybe you're one of the folks avoiding jumping in because they think they don't have enough money. This is reasoning that comes from decades of being taught you don't spend what you don't have. In reality, that's a simplistic viewpoint that ignores the intricacies of the real estate industry. If you've ever heard of a private money broker – and if you're reading this book, you probably have – you already know there are other ways to get involved.

In the following pages, you're going to learn both the basics and the secrets of becoming a private money broker - also known as a money connector - in order to eventually establish a passive income. By the time you're done reading the first chapter, you'll no doubt already realize how easy this process can be. You'll learn how to get into real estate without worrying about the complex issues of down payments, inspections, closing costs and the other things that scare people away from securing their own financial success. Even better, you'll come to recognize that brokering is a profitable endeavor regardless of how the market is doing.

Now, you're probably still wondering about money. Right? You're thinking, "How can anyone get involved in real estate investment without tens of thousands of dollars to buy a home." This is one of the single biggest misconceptions about building a passive incoming stream through real estate. When you become a private money broker, you don't go out and purchase real estate as an investment. You could do this if you wanted, especially considering how popular and potentially lucrative house flipping is these days, but you won't have to do all that work. I can show you a better way.

After all, if you're out there bidding on houses, knocking down walls, rehabbing properties, putting homes on the market and doing other real estate work, the money you're making isn't very "passive." This is why so many retirees and folks around retirement age get into private money connecting. This isn't to say that brokering real estate deals is a passive income stream. In reality, it's more of what the kids call a "side hustle." You are putting in work to make these contracts a reality, but it's far less work than flipping houses on your own. The best part about this entire thing, though, is that it leads to passive income.

When folks put in a little of their free time to broker deals, they're establishing a way to continue earning money long after they stop working. That's because connecting investors with those who have capital is a stepping stone to becoming a private money lender. At that point, your income can become *truly* passive. Countless "Average Joes" have also entered this industry to supplement the money they earn and create a bigger, better future. There are even successful real estate professionals who got their start in private money brokering. And if I'm being straightforward with you, the only thing special about these individuals is their commitment. If you've got that, you can succeed.

By the end of this book, you'll have an understanding of what you need to do to make a career out of private money connecting and what your options are for building upon that foundation to go even further, to make even more. Because once you become successful in this endeavor, you probably won't want to stop at just brokering. You'll eventually want to leverage your new skills and experience, roll over the profits you earn and become a private money lender. That's where the big bucks are, and once you reach that point, the work necessary to earn a passive income will become even more effortless.

It all sounds too good to be true, right? If you were sitting across from me, you'd probably be rolling your eyes and trying to find an escape plan. Let me ask one favor: get through *a single* chapter. There are five chapters in this book, and they're all packed with information that can help you develop a promising real estate career, even if you don't have the capital to start buying homes. If you just commit to finishing the first chapter, you'll see exactly how simple the entire process is. There are no shortcuts when it comes to real estate investment, but there's also no need to make it harder than it has to be.

The following pages can change your life if you let them, and it all starts with signing up for one of our seminars or funding tours. By learning the basic methods of the process - simply connecting people - you can build an income stream that sets you up for the future you desire. What other book can help you find that sort of financial freedom? Devote the little time that's necessary to read through these pages, and you'll already be on your way to bragging about "the perfect side hustle."

CHAPTER 1:
THE BIG SECRET: WHY BROKER MONEY?

Anyone looking to make money in real estate has a variety of options in front of them. You could purchase properties and then rent them out, put money into real estate investment trusts (REITs), buy property tax liens (i.e. a legal claim over a property until the lien is paid off), or even get into the business of flipping houses. When gross returns for flippers recently hit their highest point in 20 years, plenty of people started looking into this form of property investment.

If you're reading this book, it's probably because you're not quite sure about those approaches, or maybe you sense there might be a better way. While each of those options I've mentioned so far sound like they could create a decent return on investment, there are inherent risks to each of them. In fact, countless people have gone broke attempting those strategies. Fortunately, you don't have to be one of them. The real golden goose would be finding a real estate profession that doesn't require you to inject cash into properties.

There's a very good chance that's why you picked up this book today. By becoming a private money broker, you can build your way to a passive income stream without having to get a real estate license, attend foreclosure auctions, scour local property ads or invest even a single dollar from your pocket into an available property. As mentioned previously, this shouldn't be your final goal. This is just a step towards a brighter financial future.

And, hey, maybe you already have everything you need to become a private money lender. We'll discuss that in more depth later. For now, let's start with the basics.

WHAT IS A PRIVATE MONEY BROKER?

There are countless players in the real estate industry. While we might only envision buyers and sellers when we think of the housing market, usually with a real estate agent in the middle, there are actually many other roles that people play. And, in many cases, those who may seem to have similar interests at first glance can have very different end goals. Two competing buyers making an offer on the same home, for instance, often don't have the same vision for the property.

That's because buying your family's dream home and buying a house as an investment are two very different things. If someone wants to invest in a property to fix up and flip it, they often need to find someone to lend them the initial seed money. While some folks may have the capital to purchase properties on their own, and the necessary funds to rehab the home, this isn't how things are normally done. Thank goodness, right?

The problem for the investor is often finding someone willing to provide them with that money. This is where a private money broker comes into play. This book could include entire chapters on the definition of a private money connector, but I can boil it down to a simple concept. This form of capital connecting is simply *finding somebody who needs cash, and finding someone who has cash, and just bringing the two of them together.*

It seems like a simple concept, and that's because it is. Once you know how to put these deals together, doing so can be as easy as placing a few phone calls. The best part is that private money brokers are compensated generously for their time. Lenders need a place to invest their money to turn a profit, and buyers need that money so they can turn a profit themselves. By bringing these parties together, private money connectors are providing an invaluable, connective service.

THE START OF AN ENTERPRISE

When people learn what it is that a private money broker does, they often have trouble initially wrapping their head around the concept. After all, it sounds like those who get involved are making money off real estate without purchasing it, loaning money on it or doing any other typical form of investment. In fact, it sounds like they can do all of this from the comfort of their home without spending a dollar on the deals they're brokering.

If this is what it sounds like to you, it's because that's exactly how it works. In fact, there has been a surge in the number of private money connectors in recent years. The increased availability of technology to work from home and an economy where "side hustles" became the new norm opened countless peoples' eyes to what they were missing out on. Of the many success stories that could be told of these individuals, the best way to really describe this career path is to tell the story of one of the biggest players in the industry. My story.

Humble Beginnings

Once you hear the humble beginnings of The Lee Arnold System of Real Estate Investing, it becomes clear that literally anyone with a basic commitment to success can do this job. Indeed, the word "humble" is not an exaggeration. Back in 1995, I was 18 years old and working at a grocery store for $3.90 an hour. My shift lasted until midnight, so I usually caught all the late-night infomercials when I got home. One of those infomercials piqued my interest; it was an offer for a three-day seminar on making money in real estate.

The only problem was that the seminar cost $1,590. For a poor 18-year-old writing car, insurance, rent and college tuition checks on a $3.90/hour paycheck, this was not going to happen. Even worse, I was three months behind on my truck payments with maxed-out credit cards and a credit score below 500. I reached out for a bank loan but was turned down, so I moved on to asking folks I knew. I tried just about everyone at the grocery store, and they all said no.

Finally, I turned to the pharmacist, Brent, and said, "I'm going to be a real estate millionaire. I just need you to write me a check for $1,590, so I can go to this training."

Brent said, "Lee, once you go through it and you find a good deal, let me know, because I'd be happy to lend you the money." He actually said "once you go through it," so this was the first person I talked to that actually believed I could do this and it was possible. That was a head-blowing explosion because suddenly I had a financial backer and I'd never had that before. Now I just needed to find a deal.

All this backstory is to make one point clear: the idea that you need massive resources to make money in real estate is ridiculous. Once you become a private money broker, you can bring in passive income without spending a dollar. Of course, my story doesn't stop with a promise from a future potential investor. Just when I thought the three-day seminar was a lost cause and a missed opportunity, I received a call from the bank saying they could loan me the money by refinancing my truck.

The First Deal

Unfortunately for me, the training seminar wasn't about how to become a private money connector. But I did walk away with a new knowledge set, and I used it to set out on the hunt to buy a property. Eventually, I found the most rundown, dilapidated, hoarder house you could imagine in an estate sale.

Eventually, I found the most rundown, dilapidated, hoarder house you could imagine in an estate sale. I had the opportunity to purchase this thing for $35,000, so I signed the contract with a $1,400 earnest money deposit – left over from my truck refinancing – and hoped Brent would make good on his promise. After taking one look at the house, if you could even call it that, Brent decided it was a bad investment.

But that didn't stop me. Yes, the house would cost $35,000. Yes, it would need $15,000 in rehab before anyone would buy it. But once the house was ready to sell after the $50,000 investment, it would be worth $80,000. That was a $30,000 margin, and I was promising to do all the rehab work myself. All of a sudden, this sounded pretty great to Brent, and at that moment, he became a private money lender. I, on the other hand, spent the next six months getting the house ready to sell, while working my full-time grocery job and going to school.

When all was said and done, Brent and I cleared a $29,000 profit on the home. We split the cash and I was happy to have made some money, but I also realized that I had done all the work. Brent had merely signed a check. Right then, I decided that I wanted to be in that position one day, but obviously I didn't have the money at that time to go around lending to eager flippers.

This led me to wonder if maybe I could track down other people who needed money to purchase property and connect them with folks who had the money. That didn't sound nearly as hard as fixing up a decrepit hovel filled with hoarded items and human waste.

Becoming a Private Money Broker

This was the beginning of my path to becoming a private money broker. A simple three-line ad in the newspaper declaring, "Cash for good real estate investment deals" led to a call from a woman in Salt Lake City. She had a 50-unit apartment building and needed $25,000 for property repairs.

The banks refused to help her out because she had several liens, but she promised that the $25,000 she needed could be paid back within six months. So I got to work on building a deal. I crafted a loan agreement where the borrower would pay five percent ($1,250) for establishing the loan – also known as five points in loan origination fees – and have a 25 percent interest rate.

The apartment building owner was more than excited to sign the loan agreement. Once I had that piece of paper in hand, I started making phone calls.

I reached out to a CPA I knew and detailed the loan agreement. Was the CPA interested? In a 25-percent interest loan secured against a 50-unit apartment building? Absolutely! Once my colleague decided to provide the loan, a call was made to the apartment building owner and the papers were signed. Remember the $1,250 loan origination fee? That went right into my pocket.

What did I really do here? I didn't buy the apartment units. I didn't loan any money on the building. I simply placed a cheap ad, made a few phone calls and walked away with $1,250 for six hours of work. That was the start of my journey into the private money connecting industry, and I made enough profit doing this to become a private money lender, while also purchasing properties to flip. In the first decade of the new millennium, I had tens of millions of dollars in construction and private loans spread across the country.

And when you look at the nuts and bolts of my story, it all started with an investor who needed money (me) and a lender who needed an investment (Brent). Once I discovered that I could make money without being in either of these positions again – but rather a broker between them – my earning potential was bound only by my own willingness and ability to just bring people together.

LESSONS LEARNED FROM THE RECESSION

My rise in real estate investment culminated in the founding of Secured Investment Corp. The company helps broker deals between private lenders and borrowers, and the Cogo Capital subsidiary also acts as a private money lender. Unfortunately, my journey hasn't been all smooth sailing. The housing crisis really hit home in 2008, hurting me and millions of other Americans. It's worth pointing out that if I had only ever brokered deals between people, the economic downturn would've had minimal effect on me. When the bottom fell out, though, I had tens of millions in open real estate investments.

When everything went south, I spent 18 months just trying to avoid bankruptcy. Some assets went to foreclosure, and I had to sign deals back over to some investors. When everything was said and done, I was down pretty close to rock bottom. That's one of the risks people take when they invest fortunes. But if there's one silver lining of the Great Recession, it's proof that private money brokering can survive such downturns. My finances were devastated during that time, but then the phone rang.

It was a client. Home prices were at historic lows, and they needed capital to invest. At that point, most of my known lenders were gone. Some major players had seen what was coming and pulled out in time. But that led to the second phone call – this time from an investor sitting on millions of capital. Things had been quiet for 18 months during the recession, but they were ready to get back into the game. At that point, I had everything I needed to broker a deal: someone who needs cash and someone who has cash.

The rest, as they say, is history. My company has become one of the most successful in the real estate investment industry, and that's because the economic downturn couldn't stop the need for brokers – not in 2009 and not now. Even when you're starting from almost nothing, remember that it costs literally nothing to just bring borrowers and lenders together. Do you want to learn how to do this - even if you can't make it to a seminar? Then take a moment to sign up for one of our webinars that teach brokering. Learning everything you need to know to build a brighter future - right from your computer? I'm going to say that's what technology was intended for.

OVERCOMING THE OBJECTIONS

Whether someone wants to get into flipping houses, purchasing property to sell at a later date, or building a substantial side income through private money brokering, there's a million reasons to say "No." They might feel like they're too busy with everything else in their life or they don't know enough about the industry. Or, they might just decide that they want to do absolutely nothing during their retirement. In most cases, though, it all comes down to one word. To be fair, it's a fairly significant word: *money*.

By now you've hopefully gotten the idea that your bank account isn't a blockade to becoming a private money connector. Brokering is about networking and building relationships. This certainly doesn't mean you have to attend trade shows or real estate conferences. You don't even have to build lasting relationships with the people you work with, although doing so can be very profitable moving forward. The mere ability to track down people who need money and connect them with those who have it is enough. And as we've already discussed, this can be as simple as a three-line newspaper ad (or, nowadays, a three-line social media post).

If you've put some thought into this, you've no doubt started wondering about the people who want to flip the houses. Those individuals are half the entire private money brokering system and, like you, many of them are coming from a place of questioning, "How can I do this without money?" While you will be able to make money off real estate without any investment after becoming a private money connector, individuals who get into flipping will need money. And if the market isn't going well, you may assume that flippers simply won't be in business.

This is an understandable concern to have, but it's one that's completely wrong. Wondering how flippers could possibly do what they do without substantial assets to enter the market is okay. And if they're not entering the market, how could you possibly make money off of them? That's what makes the brokering process so perfect. Aspiring flippers look at these real estate television shows and think, "That's great, but I don't have $150,000 dollars to do that. I guess I can't." The **big secret** – maybe even bigger than how simple it is to become a private money broker – is that these individuals *don't need* major investments. This isn't even something you need to learn at one of our seminars.

Because lenders like Cogo Capital need to invest their money somewhere. Otherwise, they're not making money themselves. This brings us to the second concern of aspiring flippers: "I don't know how to find a dealer or negotiate." That's where you come in, as the broker. You're the one who is going to bring them the money they need, and in doing so, you're going to help a lender turn a substantial profit. Once you realize these basic tenets of real estate, it becomes very obvious how so many people make so much money through private money connecting.

Your biggest concern might now revolve around how you find these people. Sure, Craigslist can help. There are many better ways, though, to find investors. This is what we want to show you with our proven system. Tracking down investors is a simple process, and it's allowed us to raise droves of money. That money is with our subsidiary Cogo Capital, and it's just sitting there waiting for investors to take it. Do you know the old saying *"your money should be working for you"*? If it's not, you're losing money. We have money sitting around collecting dust, and until it gets placed with an investor, it's not doing anyone any good. That's why we need *you* to bring us investors.

You could obviously try out banks and some other financial institutions, but they'll require flippers to have money in their accounts.

This isn't the case for private money lenders. Because they're not investing in a specific person; they're investing in a great real estate deal. This means neither you nor the buyer you're working with will need to start with substantial capital. If someone can find a motivated seller, you can bring them to a motivated lender. And when future real estate professionals bring the objections we mentioned to you, you now have the knowledge to put them on the right track.

That's how easy private money brokering can be. For every person involved in these deals – including the buyer, the broker, and the lender – the sky's the limit. What are you waiting for? Sign up for one of our seminars, funding tours or brokering webinars now and learn how to start making real money.

A WORD OF CAUTION

So, you've made it to the end of the first chapter and, in the introduction, you were promised that by this point you'd understand how simple the private money brokering process can be. Have you gotten to that point? Are you ready to hop on the phone and start making thousands of dollars one a single deal? Before you toss the rest of this book aside and start placing ads all over the internet, though, it's important to heed a word of caution.

While private money connecting can be a very lucrative profession, especially for those who use it as a catapult into private lending and other real estate careers, it's important that you don't try to do this without proper legal and financial advice.

As we'll discuss in later chapters, discovering and leveraging great deals is as simple as running down a checklist and ensuring that a property meets all the requirements. I'll tell you what those are, but if you don't know what you're looking for, there's no way to recognize what is a good deal and what isn't. Signing your name to a loan – or making a loan yourself – is a binding legal agreement. If you do this without knowing the right procedure, or without help from a company like Secured Investment Corp., you'll be taking a major risk without any understanding of what's involved.

Becoming a private money broker sounds simple and, in reality, it is. Once you're trained in this area, brokering deals is truly an easy, straightforward and rewarding thing to do. When you look behind the scenes, though, you'll find a lot of moving parts. Just overlooking one of the crucial checkboxes can be detrimental, even disastrous. You can lose a lot of money doing this.

So, take the time to finish reading my book. And when you decide to become a private money connector, make sure you do it the right way. I want you to succeed.

Secured Investment Corp. is a great place to start, but even if you don't go that route, make sure you get help from finance experts in real estate, mortgages and general accounting. No one should have to lose money simply because they weren't fully informed on the intricacies of private money brokering – particularly when you consider how simple the process really is. Go ahead and sign up for one of our seminars to better prepare yourself for whatever route you choose to go.

CHAPTER 2:
AN UNPRECEDENTED OPPORTUNITY

D id I deliver or did I deliver? Now that you've made it through the first chapter of this book, you have a basic understanding of how private money connecting works. You know that your success depends more upon bringing together the right people, rather than having a large nest egg in the bank or a skill for rehabbing old houses. You know that the entire process is simple, even if you need a little bit of training on how to get started and what to look for. And, most importantly, you know that there are private lenders out there who want to put their money into real estate investments. Fortunately, you'll be able to help them soon enough.

The big question most people have at this point is *Why now?* Far too many individuals let great opportunities in their life slip by simply because they thought there would be more time later. Think back to anything you've regretted or wished you'd pursued in your life and one thing will become apparent: there's always a million reasons not to do something. While it would be great if a simple proverb or inspirational quote could convince people that now is the time to do something, it rarely works out that way.

I'm that way too. I am not somebody who changes when I see the light. I'm somebody who changes when I feel the heat. If I don't get third-degree burns from something, I'm not going to be compelled or motivated to take action. But that's why I'm writing this book for you.

This chapter will focus entirely on why now is the right time to become a private money broker. And whether you're reading this during an insanely hot housing market or at some point when things may have cooled down significantly, the moral of the story will not change. Now is the right time to become a broker, because waiting on the sidelines while other people make money in the industry simply isn't acceptable.

HOT MARKETS, COLD HARD CASH

Many people are looking for specific reasons to jump into the real estate market. They want to be told exactly when and why and how and be assured it's a sure thing. But what if I told you that there's *always a reason* to get involved and make money in real estate, but that most people just don't recognize the signs? In reality, it's a simple concept to understand once it's explained.

If you're reading this during a housing boom, for instance, you'll realize that people are spending crazy amounts of money to own homes. One house in San Francisco recently sold for one million dollars more than its asking price, and while that's San Francisco, the trend is true to different degrees across the country. If you're reading this book, it's because you realize there's money to be made in the market. Why shouldn't you be someone who's making it?

Looking at the same time period but outside of the housing market, a broader economic picture emerges that points even more strongly to why you should become a private money connector. About one-fifth of all dollars in circulation were recently printed during *a single year*. The government was desperate to breathe life back into the economy amid the pandemic, and this led to unprecedented levels of new money being pumped into circulation. While this may save the overall economy, it has a singular effect on your financial situation: your money decreases in value.

Of course, this is nothing new. Inflation is a constant and consistent reality in our world. If you go back to 1975, something that cost one dollar would now set you back $4.92. Going by the same inflation rate, the average price of a home in 1975, approximately $39,000, should only be around $200,000 today.

Selling prices, however, tell a different story. Recent statistics show an average sale price of a home reached more than $400,000. If nothing else, this shows that real estate is the only thing that can hedge against inflation and devaluation of the dollar. If you're working a typical job and renting an apartment, the reality is that you're losing money every single day.

And if you're not working and have no passive income flowing in, you're basically at the mercy of complex economic forces that no one can control. It's time to take control by making connections. The average price of a home in America is around $380,000, and recent statistics show that flippers make an average profit of $66,000 per flip. This is a major incentive for folks to get into this line of work, and they need money to do so. Unfortunately, there simply aren't enough brokers to connect them to capital. Why shouldn't you be the one making money by doing this?

Do you want to be one of those people? It only takes a couple minutes to sign up for one of our seminars - a couple minutes to change the trajectory of your life. There's literally no excuse for waiting.

EVERYTHING CHANGES AS NOTHING CHANGES AT ALL

It's easy to point out relevant reasons why now is the perfect time to become a private money broker. And when you consider historical inflation, a compelling argument could be made for just about any point in time. But this really comes down to a basic primal directive. Humans need very few things to survive. Food, water and shelter are pretty much it. People have always had to live somewhere, and that's exactly why real estate isn't something new – even if it is newly exciting and rewarding for many people.

The fluctuations of the market can cause chaos in the economy, but people still need somewhere to live. Even when the housing bubble burst in 2008, people still made moves in the industry. With the cost of property sinking like a stone, flippers could come in and make a stellar investment while waiting for prices to recover. Fast forward about 13 years, when home purchases have gone through the roof, and very little has changed. People find success when they know how to make the system work for them.

On top of that, there are always going to be people who need money in the brokering world. Investors will always need capital.

This means there's never really a prime time to get into this - there's *always* a universal need to make money in the real estate space. Even during the Great Recession, brokering is actually what saved my business and helped me float through to take advantage of the eventual economic recovery.

Therein lies the reason why now is your unprecedented opportunity to become a private money connector. Simply ask yourself why you're waiting to merge onto the housing highway, while countless others make millions in profit every single day. Brokering deals between people who need money and those who have it will serve as a solid start, and if you never move past that point, you can still have a steady income to supplement whatever money you already have.

But there's something bigger on the horizon, and that's what makes this moment unprecedented. It's interesting that the title of this profession includes the word *"broker"* – because if you aren't investing in real estate, you're becoming *broker* every day. Then, once you've made enough money, you can become a private money lender and start seeing returns on investment that dwarf the size of your broker checks.

So, why is this the right time? Because it's always the best time to hedge your bets when it comes to making sure you have multiple streams of income. The last several years have taught us that the almighty J-O-B is not necessarily the cushion we always thought it would be, so you need to have extra streams of income, and that's what brokering can be. Don't let "I can do this tomorrow" turn into "I can do this next week/month/year." The simplicity, urgency and immensity of this opportunity demands decisive action.

Are you ready to take that action? Because every moment that you wait is simply money flying out the window and into someone else's pockets.

THERE'S NO REASON TO WAIT

You know how easy it is to get started and you know why you should get started. The big question now is, Do you have what it takes to get started? This isn't a question of whether you have the motivation – although that's admittedly important – but rather of, Do you have the resources needed to get started? If you managed to find this book, then the answer is almost assuredly "yes." Do you have a computer? Do you have internet access? Do you have a phone? Most importantly, can you follow a checklist?

While this might come off as a bunch of "Well, obviously" questions, the truth is that these are really the only qualifications necessary for becoming a private money broker. In fact, the entire system can be broken down to five steps:

1. Finding a borrower.

2. Submitting documents.

3. Finding a lender.

4. Closing the loan.

5. Getting Paid.

The following chapters will dive into each of these steps and the entire proven process of private money connecting, introduce you to real people who found success in this work, and help you create a 29-day action plan for changing your life for the better. Do you want more money in your life to enjoy the things you love? Are you tired of working nonstop for peanuts or just sitting back watching your money lose value as more dollars are pumped out of the treasury? Whether you're a retiree looking for supplemental income or a blue-collar worker looking to change the game, you'll find opportunities in the pages ahead.

If you decide private money brokering isn't for you once you've finished reading, try your best to still use this information to at least purchase a home of your own. Even if you're getting a cost of living raise every year at your job, it simply can't keep up with inflation and rising real estate values. Without owning property, you're merely getting broker by the day. The following pages hold priceless information for brokers and lenders that can change your life, and once you sign up for one of our seminars, you'll have a set of knowledge that most people spend countless dollars for while they try to get a degree that they really don't need. But if you decide it's not for you, you can still use what you've learned to live a little better.

Regardless of the direction you go, your first step should be to the pages ahead.

CHAPTER 3:
INSIDE THE PROVEN PROCESS

I f you've made it this far in our book, you're
exactly the type of person who can benefit from the
Lee Arnold System of Real Estate Investing. Now
it all comes down to strategy. Your goal as a broker
should always be to become a private money lender,
because it's more lucrative and rewarding, but you've
got to start somewhere, right? When I discuss the
process with folks, I tell them they're starting out as a
broker because "right now, there's nobody broker than
you." With the proven process, though, that doesn't
really matter. When you're using my system, you have
access to all the capital you could ever need.

This means you don't have to go out and find new
pools of finances. When ordinary people jump into the
game of private money connecting on their own, they
often have to venture out into the world and create
brand new relationships with strangers. If you're using
the Lee Arnold System, though, those relationships are
already established for you. Even better, you're
working with Cogo Capital, which means you actually
have hundreds of millions of dollars at your disposal.
All you have to do is find the deals. And as long as
there are people who need money for real estate, you'll
never have a shortage of those.

When working with us, you don't have to worry about where the money is coming from. But whether you're on our team or venturing out on your own, you still need to know what a good deal looks like. Someone could call my office and say, *"Hey, Lee, I've got this amazing deal. And it's a three-bedroom, two-bath, 1,400-square-foot place, blah, blah, blah."* All that information is nice, but it's not necessary. The two most important considerations in this game are: 1. How much the home costs, and 2. How much it's worth. If it's worth $200,000 and they're paying $185,000, they're likely to be excited about a $15,000 profit margin.

"When your investor sells the home, they'll often have to pay closing costs that equate to 5 percent of a home's value. And since low-end repairs on a flip typically cost between $5,000 and $8,000, a $15,000 profit margin can quickly turn into a loss."

In reality, this isn't a good deal at all. It's only a 7.5 percent reduction off the retail price. And when you consider the fact that unexpected repair costs and price fluctuations are probable, this "great investment" could quickly turn into a loss. What lenders want to hear in these conversations is that the house *will be worth $200,000*, but that it's currently being picked up for $85,000. Now you've got my attention, and the important questions will follow.

Where's the property located? How big is it? How much rehab is necessary? How much will it cost to make it worth $200,000?

Imagine you're receiving the phone call discussed above. Would you have been excited about a $15,000 profit margin? What if it was $20,000? How about $25,000 or $30,000? We'll discuss the answer to this question – along with why even a potential $100,000 profit might still not be a good move – later on in the section ***What Does a Good Real Estate Deal Look Like?*** Before we get to that point, though, it's important that you know the five simple steps to brokering a real estate deal. Once you understand these basics and the telltale signs of great real estate, you'll have everything you need to make some money in the industry.

You can take a few moments to sign up for one of our seminars ***right now*** to learn more about becoming a money connector, but use the next chapter in order to get ahead of the game. When you know this information going in, you've done most of the hard work already.

5 STEPS OF BROKERING A REAL ESTATE DEAL

When was the last time you cashed a check by helping someone? Private money connection allows you to do just that. Brokering private money is one of the easiest and most rewarding careers available. Virtually anyone can do it. You work as a conduit for people who have money (like Cogo Capital) and people who need money (real estate investors). Every time you successfully close a loan package – and we make it easy – you'll receive an origination fee as compensation

for your highly sought-after services.

Whether you're using the Lee Arnold System of Real Estate Investing or putting in the gargantuan amount of work to broker deals on your own, the steps are still the same. Even if you choose to go no further in the system than reading this book, you'll at least know the basic journey involved in the brokering process.

Keep in mind that these steps will only prove profitable if you know what a good real estate deal looks like. So if you plan on running out and getting started on your own – which, as we mentioned, should include consulting with financial and real estate experts – make sure you finish this chapter so you can spot great deals when they're brought to you.

Step 1: Find A Borrower

This should be obvious. You need to find two parties to broker a real estate deal, and the borrower is one of those parties. There are many ways to go about doing this, and after reading how I got started, you already know that a simple internet advertisement is a viable option (whether it's Craigslist or one of the many other sites we'll show you). There are lots of ways to find borrowers, and we'll teach all of them to you through the Lee Arnold System of Real Estate Investing.

Step 2: Submit Documents

Nothing in real estate is official until it's in writing. You'll need to gather a purchase contract, preliminary title report, two forms of identification and all other necessary agreements and documents together to broker the deal. This will formalize everything on the borrower's end and contain all the information they need regarding their loan. This is also the step that legally secures your broker fee.

Step 3: Find A Lender

When someone enters the money connection business on their own, finding a lender is one of their toughest tasks. Even if you've put together a great deal, just finding someone with enough capital to fund the borrower's dream can prove difficult and time-consuming. You can try to find people willing to make these loans by attending local real estate investment association (REIA) meetings, checking websites specific to investing, talking to real estate agents who work with investors, or simply typing "private money lenders" along with your city and state into Google.

Instead of going through this tedious and sometimes unfruitful task, though, why not take advantage of the Lee Arnold System's connection to Cogo Capital? Through our private money lending company, you'll have thousands of willing private money lenders and hundreds of millions in reserve capital. If this option had existed when I got my start in private money brokering, a lot of things would've been much easier for me!

Step 4: Close The Loan

You've found a borrower. You've found a lender. Those are literally the only two things you need as a money connector. So, once you've got the necessary documentation and a lender willing to invest, all that's left is to close the loan. This is something you could have a bank or accountant handle, but you're losing money by going that route. If you're working with us, you'll learn an easy step-by-step system that allows you to handle this important aspect all on your own.

Step 5: Get Paid

Okay, closing the loan might not be the last step. You can't forget the most exciting part: *getting paid.* If you're brokering on your own and correctly crafted the loan documentation, you need to make sure you know who's paying you. When you use the Lee Arnold System and get a lender through Cogo Capital, though, we already add your fee to the private money loan quote. The moment the loan closes, you get a broker check.

SIMPLE, RIGHT?

You've been told nonstop since the first page of this book that becoming a private money broker is simple. If you look at the five steps of money connecting, it couldn't be more clear how true this is. In fact, it's really only four steps. Get Paid is just the natural, and well-deserved, result of following the other four steps.

Now that you've nailed down the essential steps, it's time to get down into the nuts and bolts of things. Knowing how to spot and act on a real estate deal that's actually valuable is going to blast your profit potential into the stratosphere.

WHAT DOES A GOOD REAL ESTATE DEAL LOOK LIKE?

If you take away nothing else from this book, knowing how to recognize a good real estate deal is the one to remember. This knowledge can save you a lot of time, money and headaches. First, you need to stop thinking about whether certain amounts of profit margin are worth your time. Instead, let's pick a margin that most everyone would agree is a great investment. Let's say a flipper contacts you about a home they've found for $1 million that will be worth $3 million when it's fixed up and put on the market. That's a no brainer, right?

Unfortunately, that's not the case. While you might think that a $2 million profit margin is exactly what a lender is looking for, they're actually far more concerned about the safety of their investment. You'll see in one of the later sections, on FHA Caps, why this impressive potential profit still doesn't necessarily qualify as a good real estate deal.

If you can find properties that fit the following criteria, though, you've got an excellent shot at being able to act as a successful money broker between an investor and lender. And if you bring deals that fit inside these parameters to our Cogo Capital funding source, you can expect to find immediate funding for your investor 99.9999% of the time.

Your success is paramount to our success! We work with Brokers nationwide and value you and your clients as a cornerstone to our growing business. Because our scope is wide and our parameters are creative, we can cherry-pick some of the most profitable fruit off the "funding tree," which means you now have a powerful friend in the lending business!

Residential vs Commercial vs Industrial

Are there great deals to be had on commercial and industrial properties? Absolutely. Are most lenders going to get excited about offering loans on these properties? Absolutely not. There are plenty of concerns we could list about the dangers of investing in commercial and industrial buildings.

Instead of diving into these complexities, though, let's just focus on the fact that *everyone* needs a home. Not everybody needs a commercial property. Not everybody needs an industrial warehouse. But what percent of the population needs somewhere to live? *An even 100 percent*. If an investor gets money to buy a home, there's a market out there for them to sell it.

Single Family vs. Multiple Units

It would be great if focusing on residential properties instead of commercial and industrial was all you needed to know about getting into the money connection game. Sadly, that's not the case. There are countless types of residential properties out there. The real question is whether a one-bedroom home and a 25-unit apartment structure are equally excellent investments. The answer to that is no.

FHA Caps

It's much easier to get loans on residential properties, but for a deal to be really great, its price needs to fall below the Federal Housing Administration loan caps. If the sale price of a home falls below this cap, there's a measure of built-in security for lenders. When the bottom fell out of the housing market back in 2008, it wasn't investors who had secured FHA loans that got ruined. The people who really got wiped out were those building and investing in $23 million luxury homes on the backside of Deer Valley in Park City, Utah. Homes in this area, and those like it, became money pits for their investors.

But what do you call a private money lender in a recessionary downturn? A landlord. If the bottom were to fall out again and borrowers didn't pay back loans, it's a simple process for lenders to foreclose and take back the asset. At that point, they can rent the property out and the government will subsidize the rent via Section 8. This means cash will continue flowing even if the housing market hits historic lows.

When investors stick to residential properties priced under the FHA cap, they're making themselves far more appealing to lenders. This cap varies by hundreds of thousands of dollars based on zip code, so keep in mind that a great real estate deal can look very different in separate locations.

Square Footage and Acreage

Have you heard size doesn't matter? Well, that's actually partly true. You will want to find deals on properties that are under 2,800 feet. Any larger than that is a big house, which comes with big upkeep, repairs and other obligations. Some of the easiest properties to flip are one-bedroom, one-bath houses less than 1,000 square feet.

While these were nearly impossible to sell just 20 years ago, fast forward to today, and you can barely keep them on the market. Every day, 4,500 people in America turn 55 and 10,000 boomers turn 65 daily. Half of them are single and don't want massive houses with sprawling lawns that need to be maintained; they want something that's affordable and suits their needs.

When you add in the fact that vacancy rates in apartments right now are less than 1 percent, it's obvious that rentals are no longer affordable, either. With interest rates being at historic lows, a monthly mortgage payment on a one-bedroom, one-bath house with 600 square feet is much lower than what someone would pay in rent for the same home. And since the value of land is currently so high – one of the many reasons a good real estate deal involves properties under one-half acre – contractors simply can't afford to build these properties.

The supply of small homes on small lots diminishes every day, and the demand for these properties is at historic levels. It's easy to understand then why lenders get excited to offer loans on these homes.

The first part of every successful fix and flip is finding the right real estate property. That's why we've created this easy, 5-point guide to help you find the "sweet spot" deal, which can give you the best chance at making money in real estate, while safeguarding your investment.

At Cogo Capital we are only interested in funding projects that will give you the best opportunity at realizing success. Therefore our criteria is centered around these 5 points:

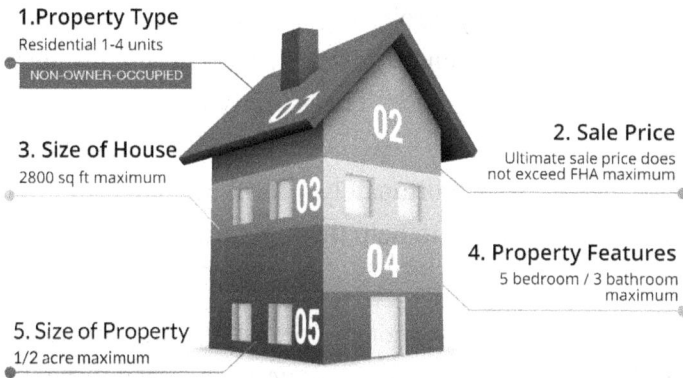

1.Property Type
Residential 1-4 units
NON-OWNER-OCCUPIED

3. Size of House
2800 sq ft maximum

2. Sale Price
Ultimate sale price does not exceed FHA maximum

4. Property Features
5 bedroom / 3 bathroom maximum

5. Size of Property
1/2 acre maximum

"I Found a Good Real Estate Deal! Now What?"

As a private money broker, it's your job to find investors whose desired properties meet these criteria. Your value in this deal comes from the old adage that, in business and in life, you don't get who and what you want. You get who and what you attract. Well in the private money brokering business, it's the same thing. If you surround yourself with people who have cash, you will have cash. That's pretty helpful since, as a broker, you'll have to connect with individuals who need cash. Fortunately, it's fairly easy to find folks who want you to help them get money.

If you decide to start money connecting on your own, you'll need to find private money lenders willing to invest. As I've said, when you're part of the Lee Arnold System of Real Estate Investing, you already have access to all the money you could ever need. In fact, because of the success of the proven process, we have vast reserves of capital just sitting here waiting to be lent out. By bringing good real estate deals to us, you'll have access to the massive funding available at Cogo Capital.

HOW DOES THE LEE ARNOLD SYSTEM WORK?

Now that you've got all this information, you might wonder why you can't go out on your own. Maybe you're thinking that it might be difficult starting out independently, but in the long run, you can pull this off on your own without training. You're wondering, Why do I need the Lee Arnold System?

The easiest way to answer that question is simply to go over how the system works. Yes, you'll find a variety of live trainings and certifications on our website. You'll find guidance on becoming a private money lender. You'll even find information on becoming a wholesale specialist, earning a home rehab certification, calculating the maximum allowable offer (MAO), and much more. The Lee Arnold System isn't any of these things, though. *It's all of them.*

My system covers all the essential facets of flipping homes – from being the investor to making the necessary loan – and it all lives in the same house, so to speak. Of course, you obviously don't have to learn all this information. If you just want to work in money connecting, the Broker Certification Training Program might just be enough.

You'll learn how to do all this with the Lee Arnold System, but what if you want to go the extra step and become a Master Broker? You'll find folks who took our Master Certification classes earning $100,000, and it's not like that's a fluke. What if you want to start flipping homes on your own? Our team with some superlative help train you for it – and then you're making money on every end of a deal. And when you build up enough capital to start lending money and creating a truly passive income stream? Cogo Capital has the infrastructure, connections, and industry knowledge to make sure your money is invested in prime real estate deals. At that point, even the minimum amount of work conducted by money connectors will no longer be necessary for you.

How is all of this done? We like to call it the Circle of Wealth. When it comes to real estate deals, there are many players involved. If you're the private money broker, you're essentially the middleman. There are the flippers who want to make money, and then there are those who want to invest in homes without the headache of fixing and flipping the property themselves. There are many other people involved, but the one thing they're all looking for, of course, is profit. And if the individuals involved aren't helping each other succeed, no one is going to make money.

If brokers don't have good relationships with flippers, or lenders don't have working relationships with brokers, no one in the equation is going to get what they want, which is to be paid.

The Circle of Wealth started all the way back when I was working at that grocery store for peanuts. Brent in the pharmacy wouldn't fund my education, but he promised to fund my first deal. Once I found that deal, we worked together so that we both earned money. That simple connection has developed into much more over the years. The Lee Arnold System of Real Estate Investing connects people via the Circle of Wealth in the same way – it's just a *much bigger* circle now. It involves everyone from the first-time flipper to the multi-millionaire earning money as a private money lender while relaxing on their yacht.

The reason people find success in our system is that the Circle of Wealth is a fundamental concept. We don't sit around and just wait for deals to fall into our laps. With the system, it's in everyone's best interest to help everyone else. When you find your first investor who wants to flip a home, you don't want to just sign the paperwork and move on with a paycheck. You want to foster that relationship.

Call them and ask how the repairs are going. Let them know you're excited to see what they do with the property and that you're ready to help again when they move on to their next flip. As the person who helped them find the money and then maintained contact, who do you think they'll come to when they're ready for a new purchase?

This simple truth holds firm all the way up the ladder. If you're having trouble finding investors, our team and your other instructors from our training programs will want to help. Why? Because once you're successful, you have a story. You are a story – a success story. From that point on, we can use you as an example to attract others to the system. Then there are the folks at Cogo Capital. I work with tons of lenders outside of Cogo, but we're all part of the same circle. If you're not able to secure funding within the system for your deal, then you're going to look elsewhere. What does this mean? It means the private money lenders and our capital company are no longer making money with you.

The best part is that the Circle of Wealth becomes easier and easier over time. For example, your first investor may pay a little more for their loan if they've never flipped a home before. This is because they're a higher risk. Once they prove they can get the job done, though, they've built reputational capital.

While this is little more than simply building trust between parties, it equates to monetary value. When your investor has reputational capital, they pay less for their loans. In the end, that means they keep coming back to you, you keep coming back to us, and the Circle of Wealth continues for everyone.

"Your Success is Our Success!"

IS THIS FOR YOU?

You've now got vital knowledge that people once had to spend years learning, training, testing for and being certified on – and that many still think they do. You know some of the innermost workings of the real estate industry, along with how countless individuals earn impressive incomes without purchasing a single piece of property.

The only question now is what you want to do with that knowledge. Money connecting isn't for everyone. We've met people who have gone through our training program and didn't have a deal months later. If you ask them, though, they'll invariably admit to not putting in the work because of a lack of time. But when deals can wrap up in four hours, how could that possibly be an excuse?

If you want to make money badly enough, you'll do whatever it takes. And this really doesn't take very much.

Money connection is a simple way to earn an income and work towards something bigger, but the operative word here is *earn*. Are you willing to attend a training program and learn the best ways to track down leads, build relationships, work with lenders and really get your foot in the real estate industry door? Are you ready to start building capital so you can transition from brokering to private money lending? If so, the final chapter of this book is for you. There's only so much motivation we can give you to get started; the rest is up to you.

CHAPTER 4:
SUCCESS! MEET THESE PRIVATE MONEY BROKERS

A re you skeptical of how easy it sounds to become so successful? I get it. The world is full of snake oil salesmen and irritating 24-year-olds on YouTube telling you to download their get-rich-quick guide. There are plenty of reasons to be wary of so-called "investment opportunities" that seem too good to be true. Most people are smart enough to know the difference, though.

This isn't magic; the Lee Arnold System of Real Estate Investing doesn't promise you will become a millionaire just by reading this book, watching a webinar or even attending a class. It requires some work, just like any other legitimate money making endeavor. But if you do put in the work, and you do try to learn, it is unbelievably easy to be incredibly successful and earn a lot of money.

Still unconvinced? I get it. You're saying, "Yeah, sure, Lee, you got rich doing this, but I'm just a Regular Joe (or Jill). Can I do it?" Absolutely! Don't just take my word for it, though; after all, you've been taking my word for it this whole book so far.

Let's see what some of our actual clients – ordinary people just like you – have said about the Lee Arnold System of Real Estate Investing, the Circle of Wealth and working with Secured Investment Corp. and Cogo Capital.

"When I first heard of the Lee Arnold System of Real Estate Investing, I was intrigued by the large scope of areas that his education covers," said Karen Ternois, from Houston. "I have been involved in real estate for several years, and one aspect that had always interested me was Private Money Brokering, but I never knew how to get started in that.

"I took the Certified Private Money Broker course and then followed up with the Master Broker Course. This has opened up a whole new chapter in my real estate career, and I find it to be fun and actually easy to do. As a private money broker, I can work from home on the phone and, in a fairly short period of time, make the same money from brokering a loan as I do spending days, weeks, and months as a realtor in listing homes, having open houses, showing dozens of houses to buyers, and maybe getting a sale to close. There is no comparison.

"The staff at Cogo Capital has been so supportive and helpful, and they have helped me every step of the way in something that was new to me. One of the best aspects of private money lending is that I am dealing with real estate investors who are actively buying and selling real estate, so the possibility of helping the same client over and over gives a tremendous potential of ongoing repeat business back to back.

"After taking the Private Money Broker course, my first brokered loan was completed with a client in Ohio whom I had never met and had only talked to on the phone. My broker fee on that loan was $5,070. My second loan closed just a couple weeks later, and I made $3,570 on that one.

"I am well on my way to having a very nice, steady cash flow from being a private money broker, and I couldn't have done it without the wonderful people at Cogo Capital."

Karen is a real estate agent with training and experience in the industry, but even she found something new, informative and valuable just by taking the Private Money Broker course. Of course, not everyone has a professional background in real estate, or even familiarity in it, when they get started in the Lee Arnold System.

Many, like Cekarri Nixon, simply recognize the opportunity, put in the work and realize just how easy it is to succeed as a money connector."

I completed the Lee's Inner Circle training in the summer of 2020 and am now a certified money broker," she said. "I just got my first check from my first deal and I'm so excited! Thank you for all that you all do over there, I never would have known about brokering without you all! I feel prepared and knowledgeable talking to clients. I'm still learning but just wanted to say thank you and I'm finally earning some money!"

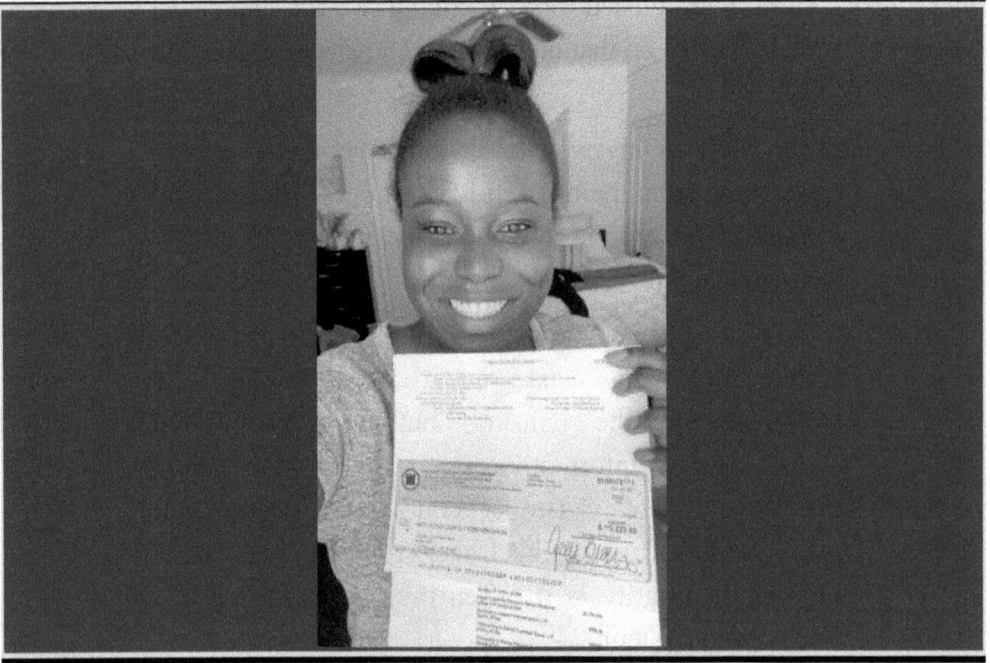

It's safe to say that, after finishing Lee's Inner Circle training, Cekarri is earning lots of money, as she is now the Chief Executive Officer at Motivated Cash in Los Angeles. Want more proof? Read on!

Here's Sheila Wakeman, who decided, nearly 40 years after earning a PhD in philosophy from the University of Texas, to get into the private money brokering game: "Since being trained through the Lee Arnold System of Real Estate, especially the very valuable Master Rehabber Course, I have – in one year at the age of 74 – for the first time in my life purchased six houses to fix and flip. Three have sold, two have contracts on them with closing dates, and the final one is currently being finished and listed on the MLS for sale. Am I proud of myself? You bet!"

And here's Lowel Yoder, who contacted me in 2017 to thank me for the "tremendous amount" he learned during a training session in Idaho. His email, which described what he called "my story from poverty to unlimited potential," went like this: "Growing up, I dropped out of school in the 11th grade. After family deaths, I remember once when all my family had to eat was peanut butter and celery. It was do or die. After Lee's Inner Circle, there was no choice but to DO. I now hold a wholesale check in my hand for $15,000 that took 9.5 hours of my time.

I also made a $70,000 profit for a 38-day rehab! I got an extra $30K profit because of the staging and marketing steps I received from Lee! I thought this kind of story was only for special people…"

That email made me so proud and happy, and after sharing it with the whole office (there were definitely some tears), I called up Lowel to congratulate him. "I haven't even cashed the check," he told me. "I like to see it in my office every morning!"

The only thing I've changed in these real customer testimonials is the number of exclamation points that were used (I'm usually all about passion over professionalism, but this is a book, after all, so some of the extra-excited punctuation was removed). Others are more straightforward in their endorsements – "Lee showed me the steps of how to market the property and find investor buyers," said Dave Bianco" – but still no less grateful and glad they discovered my system."

After connecting with the Lee Arnold System and Cogo Capital, it became clear that I needed to change to truly succeed. Doing two rehabs a year, 99% on my own and self-financed, was not going to allow the growth I needed," said John Kwiatt of Indiana.

"Through the knowledge gained, I found private lenders, built an ongoing relationship with a local bank and have become a Licensed Realtor in Indiana. Rule of 56 worked when I stuck with it, and I still get calls from letters sent six months ago.

"I have upped my game from two a year previously. In less than 17 months, I have sold eight, bought 10 and have four properties in various stages. Most important has been the variety of experiences I have gained and the people I have met."

John is now a Licensed Realtor in Indiana and said the Network was invaluable to opening up more opportunities than he ever imagined. I love rereading these customer testimonials because they really illustrate the point that your success is our success. Here's just one more, from Debbie and Normand Richards, a married couple that took multiple courses a few years ago:

"We worked very hard using many strategies learned through the Lee Arnold System of Real Estate Investing certifications and master classes we attended in a short period of time between October 2017 and May 2018," Normand said.

"We used different approaches and techniques to complete the deals with Cogo financing. This allowed Debbie and I to learn the differences between the techniques. We need to note that three of the four Projects under our control were sold using the Staging Techniques we learned in sessions provided by Secured Investment Corp. We really believe this staging was instrumental in selling our properties quickly.

"If you would have asked Debbie and I one or two years ago if we would be selling over one million dollars' worth of real estate in one year, we would have likely said "I don't think so!" Thank you for proving us wrong. We are looking at real estate much differently now. Many, many opportunities, everywhere. Thank You Lee Arnold and Team."

You're welcome, Normand and Debbie. And John, Dave, Lowel, Sheila, Cekarri, Karen and the countless others who have been welcomed into the system and found success that, even if they never dreamed of it, they certainly deserve.

CHAPTER 5:
YOUR NEXT STEPS

If you turned to this page, you realize it's time to get started on your journey into money brokering. Once you sign up for one of our live training classes, you'll have taken the biggest step in securing your financial future and eventually building a lucrative passive income. And if you're already a private money lender looking for somewhere to invest, you're hopefully well aware from this book just how successful you can be within this system. While I may have humble beginnings – a farm-born kid filling grocery bags and stocking cans for $3.90 an hour – the Lee Arnold System has become an all-in-one resource used throughout the entire real estate industry.

Now that you've nearly finished with this book, you're ahead of 99% of the people out there. And that's exactly what I wanted to provide you with throughout these pages. If you had the motivation to sit back on your own time and learn the knowledge within this book, it means you've got the motivation and dedication to do this work. And when it comes down to it, you're exactly the type of person that can succeed in the Lee Arnold System.

Your commitment, with our guidance, can help you make money, and thanks to the Circle of Wealth, we are all going to benefit from that commitment.

The most important thing to consider now is what your next steps will be. If you're reading this last chapter but still plan on heading out on your own, I cannot reiterate enough that you should find professionals in your area to help with things like loans, contracts, valuations and market trends. This book was created with the sole focus of providing value and helping its readers do something more with their lives. It would be an absolute tragedy if anyone lost money because they thought they could handle everything on their own after reading this book. There's certainly a wealth of information contained within these pages, but you can't master real estate with a single book.

GET STARTED THE SIMPLE WAY

Your biggest takeaway now should be remembering how simple all of this is. You've got the basic framework in mind, and now you just need the nuts and bolts to bring it all together. Are there people in your area that need money for real estate? Are there flippers in your area looking to turn a profit? *(The answer is yes)*. Can you find a lender and bring those people together? *(The answer is also yes)*.

In theory, this is so simple that you could do it on your own. The difficult part is learning all the intricacies on your own and forming the relationships that we've already built for you. We've made it almost impossibly easy.

Money connecting is a simple thing to do, but when you're working through the Lee Arnold System, it becomes even simpler. You don't have to worry about finding the lenders. You don't have to worry about figuring out the best way to attract investors, which is especially important considering the state of Craigslist these days! You don't have to write up the contracts, figure out the stipulations, contact people who have gone into default, repair homes to make them sellable, or any of the other headaches real estate typically brings along.

And one of the best parts? You can help folks who otherwise may not have been able to break into the industry. Of course, this helps you in the grand scheme of things, thanks to the Circle of Wealth. One of the biggest lessons you'll learn about attracting investors is that our lenders are not investing in the person. Many lenders are going to look at prior bankruptcies, background checks, credit reports, foreclosures and a variety of other issues, all just to turn down a loan.

While the lenders we work with certainly do their due diligence, the major issues they'll look at are fraudulent activities and ongoing bankruptcy proceedings.

Because, again, this is an asset-based business. Your major selling point with investors is that they can find loans through you they can't get elsewhere. Even better? You've got the backing of thousands of investors and hundreds of millions of dollars. Each and every person in this system wants you to succeed, so we make it as simple as possible for you to do just that.

STEP 1	STEP 2	STEP 3	STEP 4
If you don't know how to broker, learn from one of the most successful brokers in the market. Check out this eCLASS and discover how to earn HUGE FEES as the money connector TODAY.	Or if you're ready to broker now, just sign up for a broker account, speak with a member of our team, and start applying on behalf of your clients today.	Visit your personailzed broker dashboard, which allows you to manage all your clients' loans in one place. Upload documents and track a loan's progress so you can stay on top of the process every step of the way!	Our low prices in the market give you room to make more. We help coordinate the closing with you and your clients. You'll get paid the same day of the closing.

Because even if your employer gives you a cost of living raise every 12 months, the dollar is increasingly worth less, real estate gets more expensive, and your rent rises. Your employer can never increase your pay enough to offset the cost of inflation. And the only way you can hedge against it is real estate. So you better get started and learn about it now, or you will be poorer tomorrow and even poorer next week and next month.

How much longer can you wait to start making real money? During the coronavirus pandemic, our government printed nearly $5 trillion and handed it out, increasing the volume of dollar bills on the street by more than 20 percent, which means everybody's dollar has gone down in value by more than 20 percent. And if you are working at a job and you are renting an apartment, you are getting poorer every single day. If you don't own real estate, there's nothing to hedge you against inflation and the devaluation of the dollar.

The only thing that does that effectively is real estate. I tell my clients, passionately and honestly, I don't care if you get involved in this thing or not, but if you don't own your own home, please use what we are teaching to at least go out and buy your first house, if you're renting. You must own real estate, or you are going to get broker, and broker, and broker as time passes on.

Don't get broker; become a broker. That's what brokering can be to you. We teach people how to do this every single month. These folks go out into the world with this knowledge and build multiple income streams to protect and build their financial wellbeing. And at the beginning of every one of our success stories are these words: "I attended a seminar."

Even if you're not working with us, there's no good excuse not to be out there grabbing up the money that's sitting and waiting for you. If you're ready to get a jump start on your journey to real estate success, though, visit our website and register for a training seminar. Sign up for one of our classes right now. And if you want to know a little more before doing so, you can schedule a free phone consultation to answer any pressing questions you have by contacting Secured Investment Corp.

Private money lending and real estate is not new. It's been going on for thousands of years. People have always had to live somewhere. And on this, which is what I call the highway of opportunity, people are making millions of dollars every single day while you're sitting over there on the on ramp waiting to get on. How much longer do you want to wait to start making real money?

That's the compelling part of this because whether you engage or not – whether you decide, "I think I want to do this" – I'm going 120 miles an hour down the freeway of income, making millions of dollars. You don't have to wait. There's no red light, green light, stop and go. Just join us, all right? The water is warm.

There is no reason to sit there and let money pass you by. Let's get started on this journey together.

www.ingramcontent.com/pod-product-compliance
Lightning Source LLC
Chambersburg PA
CBHW070357200326
41518CB00012B/2261